Everything Turns Into Something Else

Everything Turns Into Something Else

poems
Jeanne Wagner

GRAYSON BOOKS
West Hartford, CT
www.GraysonBooks.com

ISBN: 978-1-7335567-8-1
Library of Congress Control Number: 2020930327

Book & cover design: Cindy Stewart
Cover art: Richard Diebenkorn, Berkeley #8, 1954, oil on canvas. Copyright Richard
Diebenkorn Foundation

For Susan Cohen, Rebecca Foust, Lynne Knight and Robert Thomas
who gave me advice and encouragement in my early struggles with this book.

Contents

Dogs That Look Like Wolves

When my dog hears the neighbor's baby cry, he begins
to howl, his head thrown back. He's all heartbreak and
hollow throat, tenderness rising in each ululation. He's
a saxophone of sadness, a shepherd calling for his stray.
I've read that baying is both a sign of territory and
a reaching out for whatever lies beyond: home and loss,
how can they be understood without each other?
Once I had an outdoor dog who sang every day at noon
when the Angelus belled from the corner church.
She was a plain dog but I could prove, contrary to all
the theologians, that at least once a day she had a soul.
I've always loved dogs that look like wolves, loved
stories of wolves: the alphas, the bullies, the bachelors.
We have to forgive them when they break into our
fenced-off pastures, lured by the lull of a grazing herd,
or a complacent flock, heads bent down. Prey, it's called.
At night wolves chorus into the trackless air, the range
of their song riding far from their bodies till they think
the stars will hear it and be moved, almost to breaking,
while my poor dog stands alone on the deck, howling
into the canyon's breadth, as if he's like me, looking
for a place where his song will carry. Dogs know,
if there is solace to be had, their voice will find it.
This air is made for lamentation.

STOMPING ON THE THRESHOLD

Window Licker

Derogatory name for a mentally challenged child. —Urban Dictionary

It should be the name for someone like me,
someone who's spent a lifetime licking
windows with her eyes.
When I was nineteen, I was in love
with someone who left me.
Winter nights I'd watch for him
as he came out of work.
I'd be sitting in a café, nursing my mug of coffee
at a table near the window.
From there I could see him, in his other
world, as he passed me by.
I imagined then, if I put my mouth
to that window,
it would have a cool, metallic taste, like ice
from an emptied glass,
or my mother's silver creamer
I'd shine with spittle,
then watch my face balloon forward like a fish
grazing the top of the bowl.
How else can we love the membrane of the world
but with our mouths?
And if the world removes itself,
a pane away,
as it does for those children, let them lick it for us:
the TV, computer screen, bus windows,
their saliva smearing the glass,
asking nothing from the other side,
like the rain.

A Personal History of Glass

I've run into glass doors, which looks funny from the other side,
but that's the whole point of transparency,

you don't see the other side coming, don't see the skylight fall,
don't see your own goblet tip, gravid with wine.

Sometimes I want to drink the glass along with the liquid, the air.
Clarity, like citrus, edgy on the tongue.

My grandmother told me my mother drank because she loved
the shape of the bottle,

the curve of the glass cool against her palm, the slender necks,
the lovely sloping shoulders.

She drank fast, because ice too is fragile, easily dilutes, easily
deluded.

Cloudy, crazed with shatter-lines like silvery fireworks frozen
at the core.

I broke her favorites, pink Rose of Sharon champagne glasses
the color of rinsed blood in the drain.

I couldn't stop the curtain from billowing, from backhanding
the whole row, so that her heirlooms

no longer loomed in the air, but lay there in pieces. We never
finished a meal in peace

because every break in transparency shows, the way white
shows every stain.

Touch It Every Day

Someone gave it to me as a prompt—
and yes, a joke as well, but I wanted to ask
what it is I'm supposed to touch, like today
for instance, when I saw the blood-moon
persimmons hanging as if snatched out of orbit
and glued to bare December trees. I admit
I wanted to grab one of those radiant globes,
so defiantly *there*, before I remembered
the mouthy tang they're famous for,
and that chest-high crooked fence someone
long ago staked up between us, though isn't it
always the fragile boundaries that invite—
defying our fear of being caught and called
a thief just to satisfy a moment of desire?
Or is it a desire for the moment?
That's the difficult part about touching,
it's never a single thing. Eyes go one way,
hands another, and the brain keeps tracking
the time when everything veers so coyly
out of reach, like those childhood games
of tag where I was such a slow runner,
my fingers barely grazing the light
before it slipped away.

Demeter Revised

What if they got the story wrong,
and it was Demeter who first went down
into darkness?
Persephone who lay awake in her white insomniac room,
her body wrapped in a watered satin
dressing gown,
her pillow stuffed inside its ruffled
pink sham?
Maybe the daughter heard a hook grudgingly lift
from its metal eye,
then the soft wood of the screen door scritch
against the jam
before it slammed shut like a discarded instrument
struck across its strings.

What if the daughter saw from her window
the spying moon follow her mother,
her hem-torn robe, her feet in their old slippers
of slubbed cloth,
as she walked unsteadily away
from the path
to a place where she bent down to dig
between the trivial pansies
and the foxgloves?

The mother's hands raking up the dirt, taking
in their fill of darkness
until the daughter saw her pull from
its bed of earth
a bottle of brown glass
which she tilted above her mouth, poured down
too fast,
as if she didn't understand it was
a sacrament.

Maybe it was only minutes, but those nights
she felt as if a whole season
had passed her by
as she watched her mother savor the soluble heat
spreading within,

flowing from the cooler places
to the warm,
the heat she drank when she drank in the sun,
its gold transformed into liquid.

Those were the darkest times, the sounds
of her mother's curses,
the shock of her stumbles,
the tears
as she guided her out of the night,
back to the implacable room, the luminous
dial on the bedside clock
and under the skirt of a pleated lampshade,
a single bulb
shining out its artificial light.

A History of Underexposure

In an old photograph
my parents sit on the beach
at Monte Rio,
birch-slender arms
embracing
four raised white knees.

See how shyly they encircle
themselves,
the blurred gloss of their skin
exposed
to a trickle of sun.

Because this is the past and is silent,
I can impose
a pebbling of gooseflesh,
or a shiver
like the silvery quake of a film
in its bath.

Maybe the finger on the shutter
shuddered
or they flinched slightly
as it was shot.

The truth is, I always need
more clarity
than anyone knows how to give.
See how thoughtlessly
her legs are cropped at the ankle,
the way a shadow falls
across his face.

Stomping on the Threshold

It's late autumn now; the gathering darkness feels expectant, like the voyeuristic excitement of sitting in a theater as the lights go dim. On my walks, there's one window I always look into. I like its garish van Gogh-yellow light, the high-backed wooden chairs, the opulent vase with its spray of winter flowers. The table's set, as if waiting for me: a plain linen runner shows off the rippling rosewood underneath, the way a pulled-back sleeve discloses a bared wrist.

~~~

When I think about looking through windows, I'm reminded of those Sunday matinees I went to with my mother. Between the curtains, the raw gape of the stage. A room with a missing fourth wall, like a body with the skin pulled back so the surgeons can peer inside. The heat and glare of the klieg lights with their tyranny of focus. And the darkness—like the darkness where I listened to the drama of my mother screaming from another room.

~~~

How like that child I still am, whenever I watch the players, a bit monstrous in their costumes and slap. The truth is I want it for myself, that moment of being seen. Everyone's eyes trained on me as I recite my well-turned lines. Exes chalked on the boards to show me where to stand.

~~~

There's that first moment when we walk into a room full of strangers, or even friends, before the mingling—whatever that is—has taken place. The space inside the room, between the others and ourselves, is like the space of a stage before the play has begun or even been scripted. Its size indefinite, mathematically incalculable. We are like actors who are not yet cast, and thinking this, our bodies feel unformed like elements still in their liquid state.

~~~

I watched a friend, once, enter a room late. It was a gathering of maybe a dozen people, already heavy into conversation. And before he passed through the door, I saw him do something odd: he stomped one foot down hard on the threshold. After this sly interruption, this small violation of our space, everyone was suddenly silent and turning his way.

~~~

I always see it first, in the famous optical illusion test, the goblet of space between the two opposing silhouetted profiles, its boundaries shapely and exact. It demonstrates how objects can be perceived, not by their borders alone, but by the intervening emptiness.

~~~

One day I knocked on someone's door, and it opened just a shoulder's width, behind it a disheveled stranger who was once my best friend. In the musty half-light between him and the door, I saw a sofa, and on it, the lumpy ghost of an afghan where his body had lain. Door light an open book.

~~~

We use the word *transparency* now, meaning easily viewed or seen, therefore honest. A bared soul in bright light. But once it meant *easily seen through*. As if we've forgotten the medium, the *through*, the window, that can't help but take sides.

~~~

I live in a house with no curtains now. I want my windows brave. I want to see strangers walking by, to watch them as they look in. When the windows darken, I want to see myself looking back.

~~~

I remember the bathroom window in my childhood home. Woolworth tieback-curtains of butter-yellow. A summer evening when I was about thirteen. I had just taken a shower. As I cleared the glass with the flat of my palm, there on the other side were my neighbors, mother and son, staring in at me. Did I jump back, look shocked, cross my breasts with my arms in that classic pose? I can't remember—though I've remembered my whole life their laughing faces leering through the glass. Not shame, not nakedness, but the way my mind flew out of my body like a bird—flew into their gaping mouths.

Happy Hour at the Compass Rose Saloon

Walking to the parking lot after a long day's work,
I spy them through the open Dutch doors,
their bodies packed in like bees,
glassine wings overlapping,
tympana tuned in to the thrum of the hive,
these patrons who tilt up their glasses,
tap their feet in sync, shoulders swaying
in holy proximity of thirst and song.
Some swallow a golden beer, others
an ale the color of honey gleaned
from buckwheat, tulip, tupelo, and sage,
dark as the Indian tea I sip on my break
just to waken the air, to spike it with scent,
to listen to the manic roil of molecules
jostling the sides of a kettle, berserk
as bees in a bacchanalian swarm,
drunk on the fuel of their own honey.
Oh, to swing the half-doors open,
to flit through the circular tables,
to feel both consuming and consumed.
A bee in the pleated vortex of a rose.

Nine Reasons I Broke My Mother's Glass Bowl

Because fragile things invite touch. Because
glass is the complacent sister of water,

one that can sit all day and not stir, though
I was all roving limbs and running after.

Because I broke her mirror years before.
Because I was not a good daughter. Because

I watched her cup it in her palm like the baby's
bottom or the brandy snifter. Because

it was so thin-skinned, frangible and clear.
Because I wanted a bowl to keep my goldfish in.

Because I hated the neat parabola of its sides,
its wide and lipless grin. Because

when I turned it over, it became a crystal ball
I used for conjuring till it disappeared

from my hands and there was nothing at all
but shivers of glass, the air without its *here*.

Turning a Sentence Dark

It's the past tense that turns a sentence dark.
—Larry Levis, "Childhood Ideogram"

It's the action words that darken first.
Tense we say,
savoring the tension as a single synapse
feels its neurons lunge
then recoil,
recording in a binary code of joy or pain.
Sometimes light is written down in one place only,
like the final game we played
that day in Taos,
finishing our set even though a storm
turned the trees a broody green,
the smooth-rolled asphalt rippling in the rain,
the ball, soaked and slowing, awake
to its own gravity.
And just a thrombus of cloud overhead,
which meant *over my head,*
because I have always loved the darkly
beautiful words,
their language of swelled violet.
Suddenly you went down
and I heard someone say *serious,* which I took
for a second as *cirrus,*
an image passing in a slow, stratospheric pace,
then the inflected verbs began to tick
like clock hands over your white
uncomprehending face.

Civil Twilight

I think of it as *civil*, loving the way dusk
seems forgiving, deferential,

the skyline limning the Bay, nights too
bright on the Dark-Sky Scale.

The water steals itself away, diffusing
its steely gray mass,

innuendos of salt and sea-sting.
Only the hard slap

of surface remains, what the suicide finds
after seconds of falling

through the quiet contrition of air. What
is the difference, then,

between dissolving and disappearing?
Everything lost is measured

by degrees of dispersion and light.
We, the beholden,

the trees falling in the forest, needing
to be heard, to be seen.

Be civil, my mother would say at the table,
chastening our reach,

our eyes. Windowpanes holding out
the dark.

Fanlight

Everyone has their own version of the Annunciation.
Me, I like being impaled by sun shafts
pouring through a fanlight,
a numinous pleasure like stepping into the shower
half-lit.
I want wet days,
when the rain's fuddled rhythm beats on my skin
until I feel pored over like a sacred text.
I'm a sybarite waiting
for a watered-down version of St. Sebastian,
limbs assailed by soft rain.
Other times sunrays pelt me,
motes dancing like electrons inside their orbits,
light tilting,
I could almost say jousting,
sending me glad tidings that everything's
less stable, and,
oh, so much more radiant
than I once imagined.

The Ocularist Talks About His Craft

Ocularist: A person who makes artificial eyes. —Dictionary.com

We make the things we want to enter. For me,
it's the landscape of the eye.

I've studied its physics, its morphology, the iris,
where circles of warm sienna soften

inside a hard dark rim; its palette of marshes
and mangroves, mossy washes of green,

and I'm a virtuoso of the splintered light near
the center, its kaleidoscope of radial blue.

Still, people recoil when they see me holding
one in the center of my palm.

It's the fear that our parts can leave us, like
children, and take up a life of their own;

that they'll fall from us like grace, like our wigs
and our masks, our shrugged-off words,

the tight little house of the clothes. I know I make
a simulacrum, not a window of the soul,

but I keep trying to get it right. For the final touch,
I'll draw red veins the width of a whisker,

like a forger adding crackle-lines to his copy
of an old master's work.

IN DEFENSE OF GOLDILOCKS

Epistemology of the Fall

When I was a child, my father talked to me about Life,
like the Devil, some might say,
when he tempted Eve with knowledge of good and evil,
so by the time I was twelve I knew
the gist of Freud,
knew about the Marquis de Sade,
about voyeurism and castrati, hermaphrodites
and transvestites.
Still too young to know my own desires,
I knew about dressing up,
about the brag of clothes, the fib of make-up.
The history of camouflage.
He'd go on about men who pilgrimaged to the Mardi Gras
or headlined at Finocchio's,
how some would sing and sway and move their hips,
silk and silver lamé
unfurling from their outstretched arms
like the plumage of exotic birds
who turn and flaunt their bright-ringed eyes,
beguiling as chimeras, as watching the class butterfly,
lone specimen,
crack out of his stale pupa
and pump up his wings like a pool toy.
This was years before they called it *coming
out of the closet*,
years when I'd watch my mother
after she undressed at night, her real body emerging
from the bedroom closet,
leaving the woman she'd been behind.
The one in the starched sundress,
with tightly permed hair and pale buffed nails.
Her name meaning *gift of god*.
She'd sweep out in a peach nightgown,
her long arms bare,
satin Charmeuse draped over the soft pouch
of her belly,
stretched from our births, reminding me now
of those Renaissance paintings
where you see a slight mound above Eve's pudenda,

as if there's already another inside her,
and she's being punished for the sin of not knowing
only gods are allowed
to be more than one thing.

We Were Sirens

Like all hybrids, we were liminal; we were
child-women, bird-women, nobody's daughters.
We were birds of prey, we prayed to be beautiful,
we believed in seduction as a victimless crime.
We hung out on beaches and boardwalks, on
piers and sidewalks, on porch-swings and perch
swings. We milled through the parks, the malls.
At home we wrapped our new bodies in fables,
in pious cages of silk, in soft libidinous songs.
In spring we envied the swallows who whirled
like lariats over freshly sown fields. In summer
we dreamed of sailors, of sinners; we listened
for the sound of speedboats skimming the bay,
our ears tuned to the thrum of escape. We
were bird-made, were bridesmaids, we dived
down so fast our hearts became weightless,
our throats made shrieks like Stukas splitting
the air. Some heard this as a warning, some
as a wail. Still, others knew it was song.

Everything Turns Into Something Else

It's been raining all week, the air a broth
of clouds and mist,
gutters building to a slow boil.
I've decided to prepare a supper of lamb soup
and olive bread,
to simmer the shanks and neck for hours
in a cast iron pot,
the way my grandmother used to do, adding
onions and carrots, a few tomatoes
for acid and color,
putting the cabbage in last, tearing away
the outer leaves
that grip the center of themselves
as if afraid to let go.
Because soup needs the savor of cabbage,
the way we need the raw,
the heady, a bit of gaminess to sharpen
our lives.
Last week I stood by a fence and fed hay
to real lambs,
still standing, wooly shanks and all, pupils
cocked sideways,
ready to take in the world.

Why I'm Often Suspected of Shoplifting

I must look like a thief wandering the aisles,
eyes skimming over scarves,
their silks rippling like sea anemones.

My eyes in the farmers' market
stroking the golden bulge of a mango,
or the violet skin of Concords

hanging from their chandelier clusters.
In Saks, once, a clerk came up and stood beside me,
gave me a restraining glance

as my eyes ogled the opal buttons
on a blue voile blouse,
caressed its collar with all the concentration

of a back-window voyeur.
Maybe it's because the eyes are natural predators,
are orbital limbs, are feral,

are the fingers, the paws of the mind
pacing over open grasslands
with intent to devour.

The nuns always cautioned us to keep
custody of our eyes,
as if we should make them file daily reports,

wear shackles, stay downcast, stay lidded,
stay sealed like lips
that don't ask, won't tell.

I was only browsing, I wanted to say to the clerk,
my mouth full of new shoots,
a bit of tender bark, some smallish buds.

The Genesis Machine

The first commercially available aeroponic apparatus was known as
the Genesis Machine. Aeroponics is the process of growing plants in an air or
mist environment without the use of soil. —Wikipedia

I walk by rows of see-through growing pans,
embarrassed for the stringy taproots

dangling like legs with their pants pulled down.
Pale strands kinked and twiddling the air.

No soft bed of loam to sink their tendrils in,
no ground to moil, no dark earth,

origin of all their convoluted dreams.
Only a constant dose of patented mist,

like those department store perfumes
I used to spray behind my ears,

inhaling the counterfeit pheromones
to learn the language of scent, because

I wanted to learn all the invisible things,
roots unraveling like ripped out yarn,

ganglia, rhizome, folded cerebellum.
The frizzy-haired child who blamed her

misshapen follicles on the family genes,
each strand defined by the shape of its fiber:

smooth, ovoid or crimped, the mind
itself a maze, a puzzle, like the patterns

the ancients read in the entrails of animals,
knowing the holiness of hidden things:

roots a childhood scrawled upside down
in the dark—though these roots are orphans,

are clones, the hairs on the ends sucking
their potions with a finely calibrated hunger,

their leaves too groomed and coddled, too free
of growing pains to love this world I love.

After the Election, I Learn of the Rift in the Larsen Ice Shelf

I have to tell you, there have always been rifts,
even in the rocky mantle whose name
means *cloak*,
because it covers the edges, the urges,
the flows and the floes, drapes a molten center,
the crust chafing, grating against itself,
shapeshifting like an adolescent,
every change in formation a seismic event;
the glaciers
in continuous flux, waxing
and waning,
because nothing stays the same, nothing
remains unriven,

even in a place, so far from human contention
or desire,
that the plants, Buddhist in their demands
for sustenance, for the stingy nutrients of the soil,
are rare;
even in a place where the ice opens to reveal
another layer, which is also ice,
even in this homogeneity, you can find a rift rising up,
because heat,
which is at the heart of all things, can weld,
but also can melt what is whole,
tear it in two,

till the parts begin to drift in different directions,
at first imperceptibly, with hardly a sound,
unlike the crack of lake ice, which can turn thunderous
after a spring thaw,
warning you that a world
is being shattered under your feet,
and without malice,
but deep inside its own necessities,

not unlike the place
where your ignorance of nature's schisms
is waiting to surprise you,

but it's not your fault you learned the way
you did,
the way we all did,
first the Platonic shapes, then the irregular ones,
contours you had to memorize,
the way you learned the shape of the continents,
the states
whose borders seemed God-given, seemed
nearly absolute,

but eventually you learned whole countries
have been reconfigured by force,
the colors on the maps only passing geopolitical
fashion statements,
and that once a single mother-continent
split to become many,
ice sheets slipping on and off those surfaces
like changed bedsheets in a first world country
like ours,
where we are disappointed to find
that we are not one,
one people, living in a single nation.

Ceteris Paribus

Let's make a calendar where nothing is held
in remembrance:
no holidays, no victories, no saints or amnesties,
no special Sundays for fathers or mothers,
no lunar calibrations,
nothing commemorated for the way
it's different from any other.
Not the fasting moon or the crimped
winter light.
Let the souls of the dead come back
with no fanfare.
Each day sacred in its transiency.
Time, like an alien, slipping
through the boundaries
of the days.

Discussing *Useful Life* at the Tax Depreciation Seminar, I Remember a Line by David Baker

The useful life of a parking garage is fifteen years,
unless its roof is the floor of the building above it,

in which case it's thirty-nine. Office furniture is seven,
the stove five and the fax machine five. But if a machine

has its wires embedded in the wall behind it, so they ease
through the wall like veins, it can make that wall part

of the machine, thus five, as if there's a contagion there,
a life-changing symbiosis, one function conspiring with

the other because they're too close to be segregated, like
the heart feeding its blue canals, or the way the lungs

recycle breath—breath intangible, and therefore amortized,
whereas eyes, attached by a nerve, can be pulled out from

the skull like a stove from the wall, though vision seems to
take place outside the body, as if eyes are really windows

of the soul—windows, thirty-nine but twenty-seven and
a half if residential. Which makes sense because some days

we're an office, some days a home, but this moment
I'm looking out the window, distracted by a bee working

a cherry blossom as it wobbles in the March wind. Ah,
working—that tree is an office—thirty-nine, and those bees

Descartes would have called *soulless machines* are five,
like all soulless machines—but look at the way

the bee moves her body, synchronizing with the tremble
of the blossom as it shakes from a wind that soon will tear

each pink bud away from its branch, just as I will leave
from a garage whose roof is both roof and floor. *There*

is nothing that does not connect and so sustain. I feel
my hand raising up. How many years, I ask, is the wind?

The Angels

Perhaps an angel looks like everything/ We have forgotten.
—John Ashbery

Which would account for their reticence, their almost pathological shyness. It goes far to explain why they have no mouths, only ovals in the place where lips and tongues would be, where the teeth with their ungodly wrenching would reside, a cage unto themselves. Where taste buds lie on top of the tongue in a bath of unholy secretions. Think of those experiments on dogs, the close correlation between saliva and memory, which means that angels, like gunpowder, need to keep themselves dry, to be like old leaves, so finely milled by wind they dissolve into the air. If angels need seclusion, it's in nothing as wetly vaporous as a cloudbank, but in dust and dunes, in wadis and arroyos, in the canal lines of a godforsaken planet in its hermitage of space. Imagine angels trailing a scent as chaste as laundered sheets dried in the air when it's autumn outside and all the important annunciations have already been made. Once we sensed their presence in the *cluff* of old felt erasers when they were clapped together, exhaling those little nebulae we used to call 'our lessons.' Even now, we try to transcribe the messages they send us in dreams and slips of the tongue, but we never get them right. We know angels exist because objects, even after breakage, retain a ghost of their former shape and because the essence of a burned thing is resurrected in its smoke. Like children afraid of the dark, we wait for the angels to return, a thousand years from now, maybe a hundred, bringing back our forgotten stories, singing us our songs.

After Losing Her

He feels there still should be two of him now, like
Hermaphroditus, the statue they saw together

in the Louvre, reclining on its side: an alabaster slope
of shoulder and hip, sweet unsuckled breasts,

the way the body curled in on itself and made them
want to walk around and see the other side where

the soft apostrophe of his sex lay nestled against
a thigh like a dream of brake ferns coiling at the tip.

Lately, he finds himself looking for seams, soft clefts
where an embryo's mirrored sides weren't sealed.

He scans the palates of orphans in magazines,
the silent palaver of their tongues, their unhealed

mouths laid open like a flower. Sometimes sound
is just air forced through gouges of matter.

He listens to the harmonics of hardness and hollow,
thinks of the one-armed pianist, Paul Wittgenstein,

who learned to play both parts on the piano, an empty
sleeve tucked inside his pocket.

He wants to be that sleeve and be the good left arm,
or could he be the geese he's read about

who, when they grieve, sing both halves of their
old duet after their mate has died?

The Night You Come Out to Your Parents

for Brian

the scent of Clorox makes you think
immaculate
just as the stiff napkins standing plate-side
make you conscious of the white
bone china
how it's an appetite waiting for color
for its complement of gristle
and flesh
soon you'll be served asparagus spears
those gently
absurd over-cooked phalluses
you look down at
while your father tells the Liberace joke
again
and light sieves in from the screen door
pixelating
the air leaving a smudge
that hovers
over the table like the opposite
of grace.

Voyeurs

I step out on the deck, see my dog's rapt stare, his tail pointer-stiff—
a pose that's almost reverence.
To follow where he's gazing, I grab the binoculars I keep for spying
on a pair of buzzards.
One's perched on the bole of a dead oak left standing
near the creek
where two men are hiding beside a bank of willows:
the younger one's sitting on a stump,
his knees wedged apart like someone playing a large instrument,
a cello or bass,
while the older bows his head against the other's groin.
Their bodies a tableau the buzzard ignores,
his bare head indifferent to their desires, because he's
preening himself like a god,
wings hunched open, brazen as a flasher's coat.
His feathers finger the air—catching that extra bit of sun
making its way through each barb and barbule,
through each rachis and shaft—
savoring the heat we're all made from.

In Defense of Goldilocks

The social worker says *She's not quite a sociopath, though she does have a problem with boundaries.* I say she's only a child, young enough play house, to act out the roles of mother, daddy, baby bear. The police say consumption of the porridge is theft, and what she did to the smallest chair nothing less than vandalism. But on her side, I'd say she felt the blunt stab of its skeletal rungs pressing against her back. Perhaps she was rebelling against temptations endemic to the sedentary life; perhaps she was resolving her Oedipal issues with the testing of each bed in its turn. It seems the bear-parents slept separately, but that isn't relevant here (or is it?), because the bedclothes—how tellingly anthropomorphic that sounds—wrap us indifferently, the way beds always do, holding us on their firm, buttoned-down mattresses, those platforms for the sacred privacy of the body, allowing us sanctuary, if only in dreams. Sleep exonerates us, as the bears well know, because in their own dreams they pillage the sweet interior of the hives, which are no less than homes, gouging the soft wax with their paws, honey glutted in the coarse fur of their forearms, which they can't stop licking. But I digress, because as one bear pointed out on Fox News (which they generally abhor) the whole incident can be seen as a metaphor for the rampant destruction of the bear habitat. Another mentioned, and I think this is crucial, how their own birth and infancy, that period of innocence we so prize, takes place in hibernation. Mothers asleep, cubs curled up and suckling in the Eden of their cave-dark. Apart from this, all life can be seen as one great cycle of breaking and entering.

Little Golden Books

When mother asks who my favorite character
is, I say The Wolf.

She starts to frown, so I tell her how I like
to see a wolf in drag,

his scraggly fur tucked down under a frill
of lacy nightcap,

a single bead of slaver dripping from one
tapered yellow fang.

I don't tell her how I've had my fill of little
Miss Hood, her smug

blonde head bobbing down the lane. Hair
the like-me yellow of a daffodil.

Still, I want to trade my camo coat for one
the come-hither red

of insect-ravaged roses, the kind that nightly
slip their petals to the ground.

Mother says we should keep our bleeding
on the inside where it belongs.

Should never wear the scarlet that runs
beneath the skin

and we'll talk about the blood on his chin
when you're older.

THE UNDERSTORY

Controlled Burning

Remember how they set the marginalia on fire:
blades singed

from their slender stalks, nights with the smell
of cane burning in the fields,

mornings of stubble. The dead odors of smoke
and stillness filling the air.

Every engine knows its own gusto for fuel,
every heart its own garden

where hummingbirds poke and guzzle, feeding
their wings' insatiable whirr.

I think of my friend who tried to starve a fire
like a cold, like the curves

of her beautiful body planed flat under
colorless bedclothes.

They look the same to me now, driftwood
and trees white with after-burn.

Outside warm winds stir the air; stars flare out
in their firebreak of sky.

Scalded

Years later, I need rain, need cool water to
stay in touch with my skin. Need waves

to hug my flesh till it's raw, swimming
to slake my body's hunger for buoyancy,

its lechery for salt. I know how they boiled
heretics by mating fire with water, how heat

makes a beast of every element, because once
I stood by the tub and waited while my mother

ran only the hot tap, until steam smothered
my face, clouded the pane, the bathwater

becoming clearer, crueler; I flinched from its
curling heat, saw a scald cradled in the tub's

white lap. How clean it looked, as if the sides
had been scoured with an invisible hand.

My body undressed, hunkered by its side,
a small martyr having second thoughts.

But I believed then, as all children do, that
there's an inherent loveliness in clarity:

in windows, water, pure aggies, the crystal
wineglass flouting the sober table. Her eyes

blue as sea ice goading me, her voice
cajoling me to step into the tub, to "get in

like a brave girl before the water cools."
I thought if I closed my eyes, I might

stand in the water for just a few seconds,
learn what it means to *stand* something.

I watched a lattice of light twist the surface,
held my breath and stepped in.

Oppenheimer's House

There's a fence of woven wire and plain wood
running the length of our road,
graphing the green hill behind it.
A strict fence, a feeble fence, too high,
not high enough; a fence that tries to keep
the deer from their centuries-old feeding grounds,
so that sometimes I'll see a doe leap
to the other side, leaving her fawn frantic,
running along its boundary.

In the Thirties, Oppenheimer lived there,
in the house with the red tile roof,
adobe stucco, blue Talavera tiles on the porch,
built like the houses in the desert he loved,
its heat as close as he could come
to burning without burning.
I've seen old black and white photos
of him in his Alamogordo years,
a cigarette pinched between his fingers,
the manic blue eyes, a man who knew the physics
of entropy and fire, knew how tightly
things hold onto themselves, how destructive
they are when they finally let go.

My father told me he visited
the house when Oppenheimer lived there,
saw Picassos and van Goghs hanging on the walls.
In the one whose name he remembered,
Enclosed Field with Rising Sun,
only a stubborn fence kept a frenzied
yellow sun from burning the fields below.

On the Fourth of July, I used to stand
on their driveway and watch the fireworks
over Crissy Field: pyrotechnic stars,
each one a small public splendor.
Ground blooms and Catherine wheels
shivering and splintering, then fizzling out
in the warm blanketed air; the silvers and reds,

the fronds and flowers of light signifying
the explosive heat of summer to me.

All that's gone now, closed off; the fence
might as well wear a sign:
Eingang Verbotten.
The year before my father died,
he'd sneak out the door and escape up the road
like a senile Houdini,
saying he wished he'd just *fall down and go boom.*
After he died, I'd climb the hill and stand
in front of Oppenheimer's house
to watch those sunsets, best in early December,
when the sun seems to quench itself,
a god in a circle of fire.

Going for the Jugular

Which I always heard as *going for the juggler*, coming as I do from a family of jugglers, unlike some others who are taught from an early age to keep their distance when things are in motion; for instance, words flung out with such precision, such finely controlled force, they vanish into pure trajectory, filling the air with a whooshing sound like silk shifting against a woman's thighs. The art of juggling begins slowly, first with the proverbial rings, then hunting knives, tiki torches, Indian clubs with their head-over-heels gravity. Some things are, after all, a matter for gravity; they long to be held aloft, to be spared their eventual failing. But there should be levity too, and joy in the mastered rhythms. I've learned every orbit is sacred. To disrupt one a sacrilege. A nearly irresistible urge. Think of the atom. Think of the earth circling the sun. Think of the elliptical language of jugglers. Imagine working the five-ball cascade, shapes and colors melding in a chorus of motion, everything you ever loved wheeling away from you—then returning.

Prunus subcordata

Western Native Wild Plum

The plum trees are effervescing again,
nudging their ruction of buds
too close to my window,
pushing at me with a promiscuous beauty
ravenous as fire in its own way.
All the visible fissions of nature at work.
I can guess why my neighbor wants me
to cut them down,
the cells in his blood, called *blasts*,
indecently raging, while he talks about
how the trees draw lightning;
last year an acacia fissured down the center,
exposing what used to be symmetry
into a splay of roots so unseemly
he could barely stand to look.
Now he tells me I should give
all my plum trees the chop;
they've become too crazy, too rife,
spring spreading its fallout of blossoms,
but in a few months, mark his words,
there'll be wild plums so small
they're passed off as cherries, skin broken
and bitter-sweet,
their juices smearing the deck,
whole families of deer gorging on windfall.
I want to tell him I'd miss the way such fullness
makes the slender limbs loop down,
trees so rampant with blossoms they blaze,
their branches bursting like the shivery plumes
of those fireworks they call Peony,
Ground Bloom, Willow,
as if even our gardens combust.

My Father Was a Detective

Detection is the heart of science, he always said.
Listen to the way the wind maligns the trees.
Study the sheeted landscape of the morning bed.

Look for pressure points in touch: the wary tread
of footsteps, the whorl of a fingertip. Try to tweeze
clues from the dead; it's a science, he always said.

Don't listen to the words but to the pause instead.
Suspect the compliant one who too readily agrees
to smooth the sheets and cover up the morning bed.

Have an eye for absence, erasure, whatever has fled.
If a hand caresses, check for stains on the sleeve.
Detection is the heart of science, he always said.

Ransack the house, dig up the yard and dredge
the lake, empty the teacup and read its leaves—
then the sheets, the covers of the morning bed.

To know the spider, first make a study of its web;
the width of the span, the warp from what it frees.
Detection is the heart of science, he always said.
Study the sheeted landscape of the morning bed.

Argos

Coming home one night, I felt the steering wheel
go loose in my grip,
the car sluing as if skating on air.
My old dog, the one I never loved enough, running
alongside to greet me, moved in so close
her body slipped under the wheel.
When she emerged, barely scathed, I formed
a new bond with her,
traced the Braille of her bones, her dog-eared right ear.
Finger-combed her matty red fur.
When I was a child, my mother,
pissed off at my father, would remind him
how he ran over a stranger one night,
and left his body lying on the road.
I imagined my father's guilt, wondered
if it moved in like a permanent back-seat driver,
or if the years picked at the memory,
dissolving it into so many parts per million,
an amount only animals sense in the air.
I began to play detective, found my father's
old driving glove, called it "the murder glove,"
examined it for traces, drew it over my hand,
stroked my face with its palm.
I read mysteries, learned how detectives
find solutions in the chemistry of a follicle,
the deltas of a fingerprint,
how they detect poison in the cyan surface
of a tongue.
In school, they taught us Aristotle believed
that limbs and locks of hair,
the inflection of a voice were only the *accidents*,
not the *essence* of a thing, but I wanted
accidents to be who we were.
I loved the story of Ulysses, who returned home
disguised as a beggar,
so that only Argos, his dying dog, blind
and left lying on a dung heap,
recognized him in spite of his rags,
his rage.
He knew him by his scent, its molecules

telling as a fingerprint.
Weak and barely able to lift his tail, that dog
loved him for his accidents,
not caring about his journeys, his fame,
the suitors he'd soon slaughter,
or the twelve unfaithful maids whose bodies
would hang from a beam.

Walls

Walls can't stop night-blooming jasmine
from breaking and entering, can't shut out
the *tump da tump* of the railroad ties,

a train whistle's minor key turning
the lock in the door; still, fathers
build walls around their daughters,

who sooner or later welcome a lover
who'll crash the gate like a freeloader,
flipping the latch with one prurient finger.

But fathers tell us we'll always be prey
without a wall's adobe bravura, straw
or wood or bricks well-laid. A wall

that glows when the sunset redlines
it, long before the hour fathers find
us lying in our beds, our defenses

down, our fences down, we're closing
our blue-veined lids—worried thin.
But fathers warn us the roof's a flint,

primed for sparks, every flame on call.
Our nightmares scale us like migrants,
flout our fences, mole under borders.

We break out like prisoners of war
with maps that show where oceans rise,
blizzards redacting our footprints.

The fairytale halfway house a myth.
Its walls smug with gingerbread that
sickens the blood. Flight a false lure,

because sooner or later the woodstove
ingests both the witch and her guests.
The only thing real is our fear.

Watching My Neighbors' House Being Torn Down, I Remember a Line by Rick Barot

...talking about the place of the political in poems...you have to keep distressing the canvas of the personal. —*"Coast Starlight"*

Let's say I want to be done with trouble and I'm pretending
the earthquake fault in back of our street is starting to mend.

Or I've stopped caring. Maybe I've grown deaf to its seismic
urges, to stresses born from centuries of buried upheaval.

What good is politics to me, now that I've witnessed the clash
of bruising colors on the palette of their child's skin, and seen

how the cherry wood floor was scraped and scarred by the shrieking
chair of his suicide: kicking out the platform he was standing on—

throwing it over, overthrowing it. The same urge that tears into
any surface, defiles it, like his scarified skin with its ritualized

mutilations, or the ruthless gouge of the jackhammer, the gnaw of
the backhoe as it works to raze their ramshackle house, because

they're leveling the foundation without asking me, workers speaking
in another language while I try to catch a word here and there.

I need to tell them how I loved its windowed doors looking out on
the woody creek and how the sagging balcony in paint-streaked

pastels reminded me of New Orleans and of the year my mind
lived there. I know the men undoing it aren't the same men

who want it undone, but they're tearing it down and it's part
of my past, and if that's not politics, I don't know what is.

America Is Burning

Fiery Blast Levels North Carolina KFC
—Headline in HuffPost, July 12, 2019

Even here, 3,000 miles away, I can feel the aftershock
of hundreds of wishbones heated to their flashpoint,
breastbones burnt to ash, wings incinerated without
their final flight down some dark esophageal tube.
Global warming must be real, because, look, the whole
country's about to spontaneously combust. This summer
someone tried to shoot a man in road rage, the fireworks
in the other's pickup exploding in a parody of Fourth of July,
the air turning star-spangled, a bottle rocket's red glare
scorching his children's flesh. Today at a press conference
someone called a reporter a *punk*, which is what we used
to light our sparklers with, in the days when chicken was
a game boys played in cars, politics played by old boys
in far off places, plotting in their smoke-filled rooms.

The Perseids

The summer we were thirteen, we slept outside
on our fathers' army cots—
a canopy of oak and the night's warm breath
over our heads—
scared at the sight of stars falling.
We didn't know
it was meteors extinguishing themselves
in the friction of sky,
not the fixed stars coming unfixed.
Not real stars, their wayward light dousing itself out
like the matches we lit
then tossed to the ground
just to watch their fiery heads flitter and burn.
Sometimes when a star fell,
we'd hear one of those peaches my father called
Southern Flames
falling on the other side of the yard,
slashing through leaves,
then hitting the grass with the softest of thuds,
ripeness relearning its weight.
The reason we gave up rail-walking,
riding no-hands, spinning until we fell, dizzy,
on the front yard lawn.
There was a new falling to be learned.
We whispered in the dark, made cruel alliances,
fell out with our friends.
Other nights I listened to my mother
scream in her sleep,
as if darkness were a cage.
Glad now we slept too far away to hear,
glad these nights were braver,
stars transgressing, a sickle moon,
birds asleep in the trees.

Paco's Fire

It started because we wanted a fire we couldn't tame,
but a small one. We were fooling around, passing a joint.

Someone said Nestlé Crunch wrappers burn with a
greenish-blue flame. They didn't tell us that fire came

quick as a gunshot, as thunder. Dry grass kindling into
a spark, first a few flames, then a whole field ablaze.

I'm talking seconds. The hives in panic-mode, a swarm
moving like a malevolent cloud of comic book insects.

I was a high school kid, knew bugger-all about bees.
When they came after us, I pulled my shirt over my head.

No point in modesty. It was well over 100 degrees.
Bees stung and kept on stinging, went for the soft skin

on the inside of the knees. *Pain concentrates the mind
wonderfully* as someone said. Afterward it became

a story we told each other. Paco came to my house every-
day when my parents were away, though I'd promised

No Visitors. They didn't know a Mexican kid could play
that out-of-tune Baldwin Grand the way it wanted

to be played: *The Minute Waltz* was one of our private
jokes. *The Flight of the Bumblebee* another.

The Understory

*After I asked my grandmother why my mother was crying, who 'he'
was, and what he did that she wouldn't stop.*

I found my grandmother behind the house
in what we called The Fern Garden.
She asked me if I knew
what the word *understory* meant.
I guessed an understory
might be one of those underground garages
of limbo-gray concrete,
where the walls echo and you hold your breath
as you walk toward the elevator.
If an understory were part of a house,
it had to be the cellar,
where we hid out in the heat of summer,
its shelves lined with Ball jars
holding ranks of fetal plums and
unskinned kumquats.
But *understory* was neither of these.
She told me it was the name
for the sheltered greenery that flourishes
on the floor of a jungle or forest,
like the place where she was standing
under the redwoods,
tending the maidenhair and baby tears,
the kind of growth
that thrives in filtered light, fed by rain and
strained through branch and limb
till it's as thin and shadowy-blue as breast milk.
This was my grandmother's fragile sanctum,
a place where I had to skip from one paving stone
to another, so as not to disturb the sphagnum,
the cord moss, the fiddleheads, which,
if touched, she said, would be
spoiled forever.

Mission Street

Because light is a constant reappraisal of form,
the streets are always in transition,
house fronts flooding with noon
like vertical sundials or the wide open
faces of children,
their song a secret game of brightness
and shadow,
like the moods of the shops
with their doors ajar,
then nightly shuttered and barred,
because darkness wedges itself
between the boards of vanishing days,
though you dream of a staircase
leading down
to an inflorescent yard,
and of the shops themselves
with their aromas of onion, coriander,
mangoes and tea,
of everything that relishes
its own self-ripening,
like the body when it turns into a map
of the streets,
where an X says *you are here* but also
you were there,
evenings walking on the last guttering
green of Dolores park
or sitting on your own stoop,
watching the sidewalk
gradually cool, then realizing
you've fallen in love
with its smell of candy and ash.

The Vanishing Point

Even this tree outside my window
feels complete,
as if each branch in its fractal halving
is paying homage to the past,
like the dwarf in the Velázquez painting,
Las Meninas,
who stands at only half our height,
dressed in the soft luster of silver and black
ruffled satin.
She spreads her arms expansively
outward,
as if she's too irreverent to curtsy.
Her size alone deferential,
like a memory, resilient in its diminution,
and with that same stubbornness—
because tonight, like every night, I'm thinking,
what if you could come back
to me again,
framed by door light,
like those times you were about to leave
but then turned back,
because you'd thought of one more thing to say.
You, who were my single vanishing point,
like the courtier in the painting
who stands in the doorway holding the curtain
open—or closing it—
and there's so much light behind him,
beckoning to me, the way
it beckons only to Velázquez and to the dwarf,
Maria Barbola,
though they both have their back to it,
and the room is full of people.

Notes

"Touch It Every Day": Writing advice attributed to the poet Frank X Gaspar.

"Stomping on the Threshold": The Face-Vase illusion, also known as Rubin's Vase, is a famous example of an ambiguous illusion.

"Civil Twilight": The Dark-Sky Scale, also known as the Bortle Scale, measures the night sky's brightness in a particular location.

"Discussing *Useful Life* at the Tax Depreciation Seminar While Remembering a Line by David Baker": In accounting, *Useful life* is the estimated lifespan of a depreciable fixed asset, during which it can be expected to contribute to business operations.

"Ceteris Paribus" is Latin for "all other things being equal"

Acknowledgments

I'm grateful to the editors of the places where these poems first appeared, sometimes with slight variations:

2 Bridges Review: "Window Licker"

Alligator Juniper: "We Were Sirens," "The Understory"

Amoskeag: "After Losing Her"

Arroyo Literary Review: "The Angels"

Arts & Letters: "A Personal History of Glass," "The Night You Came Out to Your Parents"

Atlanta Review: "Controlled Burning"

Atticus Review: "Voyeurs"

Calyx: "A History of Underexposure"

Catamaran Literary Reader: "Discussing *Useful Life* at the Tax Depreciation Seminar, I Remember a Line by David Baker"

Cloudbank: "Little Golden Books"

Comstock Review: "Ceteris Paribus," "Happy Hour at the Compass Rose Saloon"

Cumberland River Review: "Mission Street"

Inkwell: "My Father Was a Detective"

Jabberwock Review: "Paco's Fire"

Literal Latte: "In Defense of Goldilocks"

Mudlark: "Stomping on the Threshold," "Epistemology of the Fall"

Naugatauk River Review: "The Perseids"

Nimrod: "Demeter Revised," "Dogs That Look Like Wolves," "Scalded," "Why I'm Often Suspected of Shoplifting"

North American Review: "After the Election, I Learn of the Rift in the Larsen Ice Shelf"

Passager: "Nine Reasons Why I Broke My Mother's Glass Bowl"

River Styx: "The Ocularist Talks About His Craft"

The Fourth River: "Prunus subcordata"

The Saranac Review: "Turning a Sentence Dark"

Smartish Pace: "Fanlight"

Solstice: "Argos" as "The Dog in the Night"

Sow's Ear Poetry Review: "Oppenheimer's House"

The Southern Review: "Touch It Every Day"

Spillway: "Everything Turns Into Something Else," "Going for the Jugular," "The Vanishing Point" as "Las Meninas"

Valparaiso Poetry Review: "Civil Twilight," "The Genesis Machine" as "Growing Greens at the Aeroponics Farm"

"Fanlight" was awarded 1st prize in *Smartish Pace's* Beullah Rose Award. "A Personal History of Glass" and "The Night You Came Out to Your Parents" were published as part of the 2015 *Arts & Letters* Rumi Prize. "Turning a Sentence Dark" was the winner of the *The Saranac Review* Prize. "My Father Was a Detective" was awarded the *Inkwell* Prize. "Oppenheimer's House" won the 2015 *Sow's Ear* Prize for an individual poem.

The following poems appear in the chapbook, *The Genesis Machine* as winner of the *Sow's Ear* Chapbook Award: "Discussing *Useful Life* at the Tax Depreciation Seminar, I Remember a Line by David Baker," "Everything Turns Into Something Else," "Fanlight," "Going for the Jugular," and "The Genesis Machine."

About the Author

Jeanne Wagner is a native of San Francisco. A retired tax accountant, she graduated from University of California, Berkeley with a degree in German and has an M.A. in Humanities from San Francisco State University. She is the author of four chapbooks and two full-length collections: *The Zen Piano-Mover* from NFSPS Press, 2004 winner of the Stevens Manuscript Award, and *In the Body of Our Lives,* Sixteen Rivers Press 2010. She is the recipient of several awards, including the *Inkwell* Prize, *The Saranac Review* Prize, The Thomas Merton Poetry of the Spiritual Award, *Arts & Letters* Rumi Prize, and *Sow's Ear* awards for both an individual poem and a chapbook. Her work has appeared in *Alaska Review, Cincinnati Review, Hayden's Ferry, Shenandoah, Verse Daily, Poetry Daily* and *American Life in Poetry.*

CPSIA information can be obtained
at www.ICGtesting.com
Printed in the USA
BVHW030143060320
574226BV00001B/35